NAPLAN·
Skills* Handbook

*This is not an officially endorsed publication of the NAPLAN program and is produced by Amba Press independently of Australian governments

YEAR 3 TESTS PREPARATION GUIDE
3

Published in 2025 by Amba Press, Melbourne, Australia
www.ambapress.com.au

This is not an officially endorsed publication of the NAPLAN program and is produced by Amba Press independently of Australian governments.

© Kilbaha Education 2025

All rights reserved. No part of this book may be reproduced or transmitted in any form or by any means, electronic or mechanical, including photocopying, recording or by any information storage and retrieval system, without prior permission in writing from the publisher.

Cover design: Tess McCabe
Editor: Rica Dearman

ISBN: 9781923215900 (pbk)
ISBN: 9781923215917 (ebk)

A catalogue record for this book is available from the National Library of Australia.

Contents

Introduction 1

What to expect 3

Revising for NAPLAN 5

Using this book 7

Test days tips 9

Writing test 11

Reading test 22

Language conventions test 41

Numeracy test 52

Answers 67

Introduction

What is NAPLAN?

NAPLAN (National Assessment Program – Literacy and Numeracy) is a national test that all Australian students in Years 3, 5, 7 and 9 take each year. Think of it as a way to check how well you're doing with important skills like writing, reading and maths.

What is the purpose of NAPLAN?

NAPLAN helps you, your parents and your teachers understand how you're progressing with these essential skills. It's like a checkpoint to make sure you're on track with your learning and to identify any areas where you might need extra support.

What is being assessed?

NAPLAN tests four main areas:

♦ Writing (either a narrative or persuasive piece)
♦ Reading comprehension
♦ Language conventions (spelling, grammar and punctuation)
♦ Numeracy (maths and problem-solving)

How is it graded?

Your answers are marked either electronically (for multiple choice) or by trained markers (for writing and text entries). The tests are designed to adjust to your level – if you do well, you'll get harder questions; if you find them tricky, you'll get questions better matched to your level.

What results are provided?

You'll get a detailed report showing how you performed in each area. It shows your individual achievement and how you compare to other students in your year level across Australia.

Why is NAPLAN important?

NAPLAN is important for schools, the government and education planning, but for you personally, it's just one test on one day – it won't affect your grades, high school graduation or future opportunities, so try your best, but don't stress too much about it.

What to expect?

What tests are involved?

You'll complete four different tests:
- Writing
- Reading
- Language conventions
- Numeracy

Why is NAPLAN online?

The online format makes the tests more personalised to your ability level. It's also faster to get results and includes helpful features like being able to flag questions to review later.

When, what and how?

- Tests happen at school in March
- You'll use a computer or tablet
- Each test has a different time limit
- You can use a ruler but you are not allowed to use blocks, calculators or other mathematical tools during the test
- You can flag questions to come back to later

How does the timer work in NAPLAN online?

The test screen shows a timer that counts down how much time is left. You can choose to hide or show this timer during most of the test, but in the last five minutes, the timer will automatically appear to let you know time is nearly up.

How do audio parts of the test work?

You'll need headphones for some parts of the test, especially for spelling questions and maths problems. The test includes audio that reads out the writing task and other sections to help you understand them better.

Revising for NAPLAN

Why revise for NAPLAN?

Practising helps you feel more confident and comfortable with the test format. When you're familiar with the types of questions, you can focus on showing what you know rather than worrying about how the test works.

How to revise?

There are many ways to revise. Try some of these:

- Practise similar questions
- Get familiar with the online format using the public demonstration site
- Review topics you find challenging
- Try different question types
- Practise managing your time
- Conduct trial tests

Why do trial tests?

Trial tests help you:
- Get used to the test format
- Practise time management
- Identify areas where you might need more practice
- Feel more confident on test day

Do the tests in this book match those in NAPLAN online?

The questions are similar in style and difficulty to what you'll see in NAPLAN, but remember that the actual online test will adjust to your performance level as you go.

Using this book

How is this book organised?

Each section focuses on one test area (writing, reading, language or numeracy) and includes:

- Practice questions
- Example answers
- Tips and strategies
- Explanations of different question types

Each student in Australia takes the NAPLAN tests in the same order:

Day 1: Writing

Day 2: Reading

Day 3: Conventions of language (grammar, punctuation, spelling)

Day 4: Numeracy

How should you use this book?

There are many ways you can use it:

- Start with areas you find most challenging
- Complete the practice tests under timed conditions
- Review your answers and understand any mistakes
- Use the online practice tests to get familiar with the computer format
- Take breaks between practice sessions
- Keep track of topics you need to review more

Test days tips

How to prepare for test days?

Here are some other ways you can prepare for the NAPLAN tests:
- Get a good sleep the night before
- Have a healthy breakfast
- Arrive at school on time
- Bring your water bottle
- Make sure you have the equipment you need (like headphones)
- Download and install the NAPLAN Locked Down browser
- Go to the toilet before the test starts
- Take some slow, deep breaths to stay calm

What happens if you are sick on one of the test days?

Don't worry! If you're sick on test day, stay home and get better. Your school will arrange for you to do the test on another day during the NAPLAN test window. There are catch-up tests available for students who are absent during the main testing period.

What happens if you don't feel you did well on the day?

Remember that NAPLAN is just one test on one day – it's not a pass or fail test. Everyone has good days and bad days. Your teachers look at lots of different ways to assess how you're going at school, not just NAPLAN. If you're worried about your performance, talk to your parents or teachers about it. They can help explain your results when they arrive and provide support if needed.

Stressed? Nervous? Anxious?

Here are some techniques you could use if you feel stressed or nervous during the actual test:

- Take slow, deep breaths – breathe in for four counts, hold for four, breathe out for four
- Remember you can flag difficult questions and come back to them later
- Have a quick stretch in your chair
- Take a sip of water
- Close your eyes for a moment if you need to
- Focus on one question at a time rather than thinking about the whole test
- Remind yourself that you've prepared well and are doing your best
- Use positive self-talk like *I can do this* or *I'll try my best*

Writing test

You have 42 minutes to complete the writing test, which includes:
- 2 minutes for reading/listening to stimulus
- 5 minutes for planning
- 30 minutes for writing
- 5 minutes for editing

Total: 42 minutes

You will be provided with a 'writing stimulus' or 'prompt' – an idea or topic – and asked to write a response of a particular text type (genre). The stimulus will be read aloud to all students.

In the NAPLAN test you will write a narrative OR a persuasive piece of writing.

We have provided one test example of each style and some suggestions to keep in mind for each one.

Your response is to be handwritten in the test booklet.

Ensure you:
- Write within the margins
- Follow the lines provided
- Be as legible and clear as possible
- Only use the three pages provided

Students must also write their full name, date of birth, school name and class/home group on the cover of the booklet.

Tips for writing a good narrative or story

Start strong
- Tell us who is in your story
- Tell us where and when it happens
- Make it interesting from the start

Make your story exciting
- Have something interesting happen
- Make your characters do things
- Tell us how they feel
- Use words that paint pictures

End well
- Solve any problems in your story
- Don't just say 'I woke up' or 'The End'
- Make sure all parts of your story fit together

Remember to:
- Write neatly between the lines
- Leave spaces between words
- Use capital letters and full stops
- Check your spelling
- Read your story back to make sure it makes sense

The Note

Today you are going to write a narrative or story.

The idea for your story is 'The Note'.

What will be written on the note? Why is it attached to the $5?

Who is writing the note? Who is receiving the note?

What will happen if the paper clip falls off?

Think about:

- The characters and where they are
- The complication or problem to be solved
- How the story will end

Remember to:

- Consider everything in the picture – even small details can give you great ideas for your story!
- Plan your story before you start
- Write in sentences
- Pay attention to the words you choose, your spelling and punctuation, and paragraphs
- Check and edit your writing when you have finished

Tips for writing a good persuasive piece

Start strong
- Tell us what you think straight away
- Make your opinion clear
- Let readers know why this matters

Give good reasons
- Use 'because' to explain your reasons
- Give examples
- Tell us why your idea is good
- Use words like 'should' and 'must'

End well
- Remind us of your opinion
- Sum up your main reasons
- Make your ending strong

Remember to:
- Write neatly between the lines
- Use capital letters and full stops
- Check your spelling
- Read your work back to check it makes sense
- Use joining words like 'because', 'and', 'also'

Cats or Dogs

Today you are going to write a persuasive piece.

A cat makes a better pet than a dog.

What do you think about this idea? Write to convince a reader of your opinions.

Think about:
- If you agree or disagree or see both sides of the argument
- An introduction – a way to introduce your ideas by clearly saying what you think about the topic
- Your opinions – with reasons or evidence that explain them
- A conclusion – a summary of the main points of your argument

Remember to:
- Plan your writing
- Pay attention to your spelling and punctuation
- Choose your words carefully to convince a reader of your opinions
- Use a new paragraph for each new idea
- Check and edit your writing so that it is clear for a reader

Reading test

This is a reading test.

There are 36 questions.

You have 45 minutes to complete the reading test.

In this test you will need to read each text, then read each question and choose the correct answer.

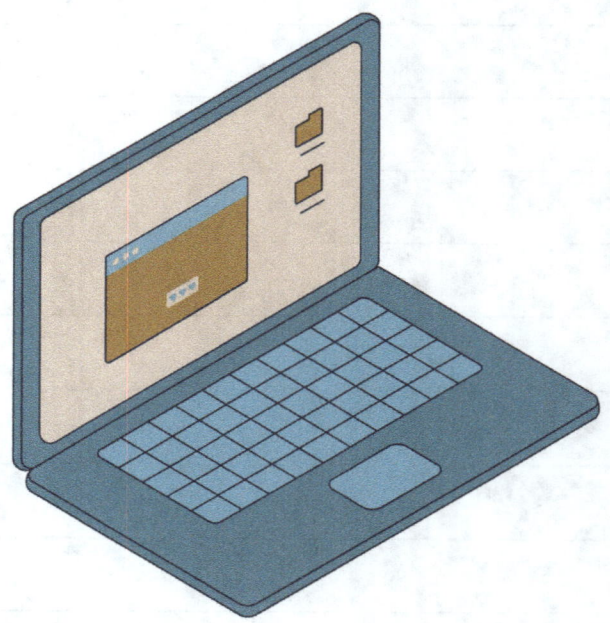

Read *What we did during the holidays* and answer questions 1 to 6.

What we did on the holidays

	'My twin sister and I went to our grandma's beach house. It's a long drive away. We were in the car for hours!' – **Susie**
	'My brother and I went to the beach, too. It wasn't far away. There were broken shells all over the sand, which made our feet sore sometimes, but we had fun swimming in the waves.' – **Jack**
	'I didn't go to the beach. My Mum had to work in the city, so I went to Kids' Club on weekdays. I went to the movies and shopping with Mum on the weekends.' – **Jane**
	'My Dad took my sister and I to the Botanical Gardens Zoo. We saw the zookeepers feed a huge, hairy elephant named Smidge.' – **Mitchell**

What we did during the holidays questions 1 to 6.

1. **During the holidays, which children went to the beach?**
   - Susie and Jane
   - Jack and Mitchell
   - Mitchell and Susie
   - Susie and Jack

2. **Why did Jack get sore feet?**
   - from playing games at Kids' Club
   - because he tripped over
   - from swimming
   - from walking on broken shells

3. **From reading the text, which child do we know saw a movie during the holidays?**
   - Jane
   - Jack
   - Susie
   - Mitchell

4. **Where is the zoo?**
   - at the beach
   - in the Botanical Gardens
   - in the city
   - far away

5. **From reading the text, which of the children does not seem to have a brother or sister?**
   - Susie
   - Jane
   - Mitchell
   - Jack

6. **How do we know that Jack and Susie did not go to the same beach?**
   - Susie did not go to a beach
   - the beach that Susie went to was far away
   - Jack did not go to a beach
   - because of the seaweed

Read *Turtles* and answer questions 7 to 12.

Turtles

Turtles are reptiles that have lived on Earth for about 220 million years.

Turtles live in all kinds of water: freshwater rivers, ponds, swamps and the sea.

They are different from tortoises in that tortoises generally live on land and turtles generally live in the water.

Some people keep turtles as pets.

They like to eat fish, plants and insects.

Turtles questions 7 to 12.

7. **Turtles have lived on Earth for how many million years?**
   - 250
   - 225
   - 300
   - 220

8. **Turtles are**
   - fish
   - reptiles
   - plants
   - insects

9. **Where might you *not* find a turtle?**
   - in a swamp
   - in saltwater
   - in a desert
   - in a fishpond

10. **The text does not tell us that turtles like to eat**
    - bugs
    - leaves
    - small fish
    - birds

11. **How are turtles different from tortoises?**
    - tortoises can be pets
    - tortoises like the water
    - tortoises generally live in the sea
    - tortoises don't live in the water

12. **A turtle would make a good pet because**
    - they need lots of space
    - they live in water
    - they are expensive
    - they are difficult to feed

Read *The ant and the dove* and answer questions 13 to 18.

The ant and the dove

By Phillip Snow

A tiny ant, having worked hard all day building his nest, was parched. He stood on the bank of a river and bent down to take a drink. The edge of the bank was slick and the ant slipped into the water. A solitary dove circled in the sky above and saw the ant in the river below, floundering for his life. The dove, being a kind creature, deftly flew across to the nearest tree, plucked a small twig from a branch and dropped it into the water for the ant to grasp a hold. The ant, clutching on to the twig, was then able to kick across to the bank and pull himself up out of the river.

Grateful for his life, the ant looked up to the sky to thank his saviour and noticed a man standing next to him, taking aim at the dove with a bow and arrow. The ant swiftly bit the man on his toe, causing the man to jump in pain and shoot the arrow far away from the dove.

The ant and the dove questions 13 to 18.

13. **What word could be used to describe the bank of the river instead of *slick*?**

    o dry

    o slippery

    o sticky

    o grassy

14. **What word best describes the dove in this story?**

    o coward

    o hero

    o bully

    o tease

15. **Why did the ant bite the man on the toe?**

    o the man made the ant fall in the river

    o the ant was afraid

    o the ant did not like people

    o the ant wanted to save the dove

16. **In the beginning of the story, what word could best be used in place of *parched*?**

    o angry

    o refreshed

    o thirsty

    o cool

17. **In the story, the ant is *'floundering for his life'*. This means the ant is**
    - running for his life
    - fighting with the dove
    - fighting with the man
    - trying not to drown

18. **What do you think is the message to be taken from this story?**
    - kind acts are repaid
    - ants can drown
    - men do not like doves
    - rivers are dangerous

Read *Onion tears* and answer questions 19 to 24.

Onion tears

By Diana Kidd

'Want to come over to my place?' Mary said to me after school today. 'Danny and Tessa are coming over – we're going to paint our bikes.'

Tessa and Mary painted their bikes orange and red and I painted butterflies on their mudguards.

But Danny didn't paint his. He stuck hundreds of stickers everywhere – there were footy stickers and pop stars and ones with funny faces and 'Yes, I am a movie star' on them.

And then he asked me to paint a huge green dragon right across the handlebars.

While I was painting, Tessa said, 'Will you tell us what your name means now?' I smiled and shook my head.

But when we rode up to the shops I whispered to Mary, 'It means "Fragrant breeze of the South".'

'I like that,' she said. 'It's beautiful.'

Onion tears questions 19 to 24.

19. **The children did not use**
    - red paint
    - blue paint
    - green paint
    - orange paint

20. **From reading the story, who can we guess is the best at painting?**
    - Mary
    - Danny
    - the storyteller
    - Tessa

21. **Where on the bikes did the storyteller paint butterflies?**
    - the mudguards
    - the handlebars
    - the wheels
    - the spokes

22. **The storyteller tells us that Danny *'stuck hundreds of stickers everywhere'*. This means that Danny put stickers**
    - all over Mary's house
    - all over the ground
    - all over his bike
    - all over the storyteller

23. **Which kind of stickers did Danny *not* put on his bike?**
    - pop star stickers
    - football stickers
    - dragon stickers
    - funny face stickers

24. **At the end of the text, the storyteller whispers the meaning of her name to Mary only. Which of the following *best* explains why?**
    - Tessa and Danny don't ride bikes
    - she does not like Tessa and Danny
    - she only wants Mary to know
    - Danny and Tessa do not like the storyteller

Read *Shane Gould, golden girl* and answer questions 25 to 30.

Shane Gould, golden girl

By Kirsty Murray

Shane felt excited and confident as she readied herself for the 400-metre freestyle. She knew she was ready for this race and she knew she could win it. Swimming was Shane's life. Ever since she was nine years old and had won her first silver medal at the New South Wales Swimming Championship, she'd been working towards Olympic Gold.

When the starting gun went off, Shane cut the water like a knife. She knew she was swimming well – she felt light and smooth. The water seemed to rush past beneath her. All her movements were precise, her arm stroke exact and powerful. The other competitors didn't have a chance. She took the lead and held it for the entire race.

When Shane climbed out of the pool and mounted the podium to receive her gold medal, she became the youngest Australian Olympic medallist in history. She was 15 years old.

Shane Gould, golden girl questions 25 to 30.

25. **How old was Shane when she won her first silver medal?**
    - ten
    - nine
    - fifteen
    - fourteen

26. **Shane's *'arm strokes were exact and powerful'*. What word could be used instead of *powerful*?**
    - weak
    - deep
    - strong
    - light

27. **The text tells us that *'swimming was Shane's life'*. This tells us that Shane**
    - didn't like swimming
    - swam in her sleep
    - loved swimming
    - sort of liked swimming

28. **Shane was the youngest Australian Olympic medallist in history. This means that**
    - no one this young was allowed to win before
    - Shane was the first Australian this young to win
    - Shane won many medals
    - Shane was the first person in the world to ever win

29. **When the starting gun went off, Shane '*cut the water like a knife*'. This means that Shane**
    - used a knife to cut the water
    - dove into the water roughly
    - went through the water sharply
    - swam really slow

30. **'*Shane took the lead and held it.*' What does this mean?**
    - Shane grabbed a hold of the ropes
    - Shane was winning all along
    - the other swimmers caught up to Shane
    - the other swimmers let her win

Read *Orangutan* and answer questions 31 to 36.

Orangutan

By Ron Thomas & Shirley Sydenham

Orangutans are great apes. They are found in the forests of Sumatra and Kalimantan. They have long, shaggy, reddish-brown hair. Males are usually larger than females, weigh about 75 kilograms and stand about 1.4 metres tall. Orangutans are arboreal, which means they live in trees, feeding on fruit, leaves, bark, birds' eggs, ants and other insects. They build platforms of woven branches for sleeping. Females sometimes live in small groups of three or four, but the males are largely solitary animals. Orangutans live a fairly nomadic life, travelling about as they search for food. Females rarely come down from the trees, but males sometimes travel along the ground.

After mating, females are pregnant for about nine months. They give birth to usually one, but sometimes two, young.

Orangutans are endangered because their forest habitats are being destroyed, and because they have been hunted and sold as pets. Humans are their only enemy. It is estimated that there are only about 25,000 left in the wild.

Rehabilitation centres have been set up in Sumatra and Kalimantan in an attempt to save Asia's only great ape. Here, orangutans that have been kept in captivity as pets are taught the skills needed to survive in the wild. The animals are studied and treated for illness. The rehabilitation centres encourage visitors as part of a program to raise awareness about these endangered animals.

Orangutan questions 31 to 36.

31. **The text describes orangutans as *arboreal*. This means that orangutans**
    - live in caves
    - live in captivity
    - live in trees
    - are not real

32. **Male orangutans**
    - live in groups
    - stay in the trees
    - are solitary
    - weigh about 100 kilograms

33. **Orangutans are an *endangered* species. This means that orangutans**
    - are dangerous
    - are kept in captivity
    - are in danger
    - are lonely

34. **In Sumatra and Kalimantan some orangutans are kept in rehabilitation centres. They are kept in these centres**
    - to be sold later as pets
    - to learn to be nomadic
    - to learn survival skills
    - to protect humans

35. **Orangutans do *not* eat**
    - leaves
    - birds' eggs
    - insects
    - birds

36. **Which of the following statements about orangutans is *incorrect***
    - males usually weigh more
    - females usually stay up in the trees
    - orangutans only have one enemy
    - females usually give birth to lots of young

Language conventions test

This is the language conventions test (which covers spelling, grammar and punctuation).

There are 50 questions.

You have 45 minutes to complete the language conventions test.

There will be a mix of question types including:

- Multiple choice
- Short answer
- Error identification/correction
- Fill in the blank/missing word

The test typically starts with spelling questions before moving into grammar and punctuation. You need to identify errors and show your understanding of correct language usage through these various question formats.

Spelling

The spelling mistakes in these sentences have been circled. Write the correct spelling for each circled word in the box.

1. His shirt is made of (coton).

2. Please (cloze) the door.

3. Jenna went (shoping) today.

4. We waited (abowt) an hour for the bus.

5. Mum (parkt) the car.

6. Suki doesn't like (lizerds).

7. Possums like eating (appels).

8. Everyone thinks Anna is (pritty).

9. Brendon (kiked) the ball.

9.

10. Peter is (cuming) to my party.

10.

The spelling mistakes on these labels have been circled. Write the correct spelling for each circled word in the box.

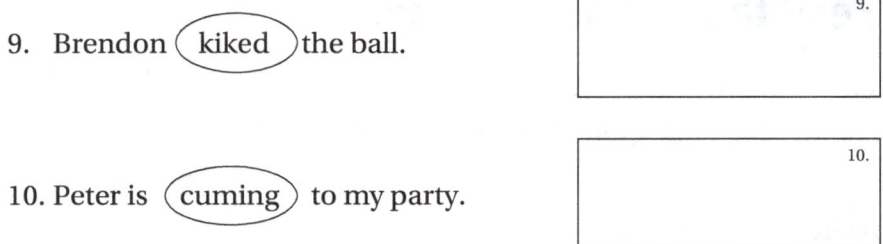

13. long (wiskers)

13.

14. padded (pors)

14.

11. big (tale)

11.

12. black (strips) of fur

12.

Language conventions test 43

Read the text about *Anna*.

**Each line has one word that is incorrect.
Write the correct spelling of the word in the box.**

Anna

15. Anna coud not wait until her next

16. birthday becorse her mum had

17. promist to get her some new

18. cloths. She was very excited.

Read the text about *Cows*.

Each line has one word that is incorrect.
Write the correct spelling of the word in the box.

Cows

19. By makeing milk to have for

20. our brekfast, cows are very

21. useful animels to cattle farms.

Read the text about *The Visit*.

Each line has one word that is incorrect.
Write the correct spelling of the word in the box.

The Visit

22. My parrents have been waiting

23. a very long time for my unkle to

24. visit us. They allways talk about him

25. and are exited to see him again.

Grammar and punctuation

26. Which of the following correctly completes the sentence?

   Penny is _____ by the window.

sit	sitting	sat	sitted
○	○	○	○

27. Which of the following correctly completes the sentence?

   Dad threw the ball at _____ .

she	hers	herself	her
○	○	○	○

28. Which of the following correctly completes the sentence?

   I am going to Devon's house _____ .

yesterday	tomorrow	last Saturday	before today
○	○	○	○

29. Shade one bubble to show where the missing comma (,) should go.

   Jo likes steak chips and salad for dinner.
       ↑   ↑ ↑   ↑
       ○   ○ ○   ○

30. Which of the following correctly completes the sentence?

   The dinner will be cooked _____ an hour.

on	with	at	in
○	○	○	○

31. Shade one bubble to show where the missing full stop (.) should go.

    Jess had a blue and yellow bike Jenny thought it looked very nice.
        ↑   ↑   ↑   ↑
        ○   ○   ○   ○

32. Which of the following correctly completes the sentence?

    He leaned his bike _____ the wall.

against	on	into	over
○	○	○	○

33. Which of the following correctly completes the sentence?

    The book, _____ was green, belonged to the library.

who	what	which	why
○	○	○	○

34. Which of the following has the correct punctuation?

    ○ John is ten years old. He reads magazines about cars.
    ○ John is ten years old he reads magazines about cars.
    ○ John is ten years old. He reads magazines. About cars.
    ○ John is ten years old. he reads magazines about cars.

The writing below has some gaps.
Choose the best option to fill in each of the gaps.
Shade the bubble to show your answer.

35. Everything is beautiful in the summer

- . ○
- , ○
- ? ○
- ! ○

36. except ____ the flies. No matter how

- with ○
- for ○
- in ○
- to ○

37. hard I try to keep ____ out of the house

- them ○
- it ○
- they ○
- those ○

38. they manage to sneak ____ . I only have to

- out ○
- up ○
- in ○
- about ○

39. open the door ____ a minute and an army

- with ○
- in ○
- at ○
- for ○

40. of flies ____ buzzing in my kitchen.

- is ○
- be ○
- am ○
- are ○

41. Which of the following correctly completes the sentence?

I have borrowed _____ pencil.

Jennys	Jenny's	Jennys'	Jenny's'
○	○	○	○

42. Which sentence has the correct punctuation?

○ Do you like chocolate flavour?

○ Do you, like chocolate flavour?

○ Do you like chocolate flavour.

○ Do you like, chocolate flavour?

43. Which of the following correctly completes the sentence?

I have _____ to him before.

speak	spoke	spoken	speaked
○	○	○	○

44. Which of the following correctly completes the sentence?

I _____ living in my house for three years.

am	been	have been	were
○	○	○	○

45. Which sentence has the correct punctuation?

○ Jane, who is a tennis player, is very athletic.

○ Jane who, is a tennis player, is very athletic.

○ Jane who is a tennis player is very, athletic.

○ Jane who is a tennis player, is very athletic.

46. Which of the following correctly completes the sentence?

The movie _____ already.

has begun	began	was began	have begun
○	○	○	○

47. Which of the following correctly completes the sentence?

This cake tastes _____ better than that one.

more	most	many	much
○	○	○	○

48. Which of the following correctly completes the sentence?

He had an _____ for lunch.

banana	sandwich	noodle	apple
○	○	○	○

49. Which sentence is correct?

○ She and its brother went to the cinema.

○ She and her brother went to the cinema.

○ Her and his brother went to the cinema.

○ She and him went to the cinema.

50. Shade one bubble to show where the missing speech mark (") should go.

"Wait a minute, it's my turn first, interrupted Jade.

Numeracy test

This is a numeracy test. There are 35 questions to answer.

You have 45 minutes to complete the test.

You cannot use a calculator or any mathematical tools (except a ruler), but you can use pencil and paper to work out things.

The Year 3 test covers:

- Number and algebra (basic addition, subtraction, multiplication, division)
- Simple fractions
- Patterns and sequences
- Money problems
- Basic measurement (length, mass, capacity, time)
- Simple shapes and geometric properties
- Reading basic data from graphs and tables

1. Which one of these towers is the **smallest**?

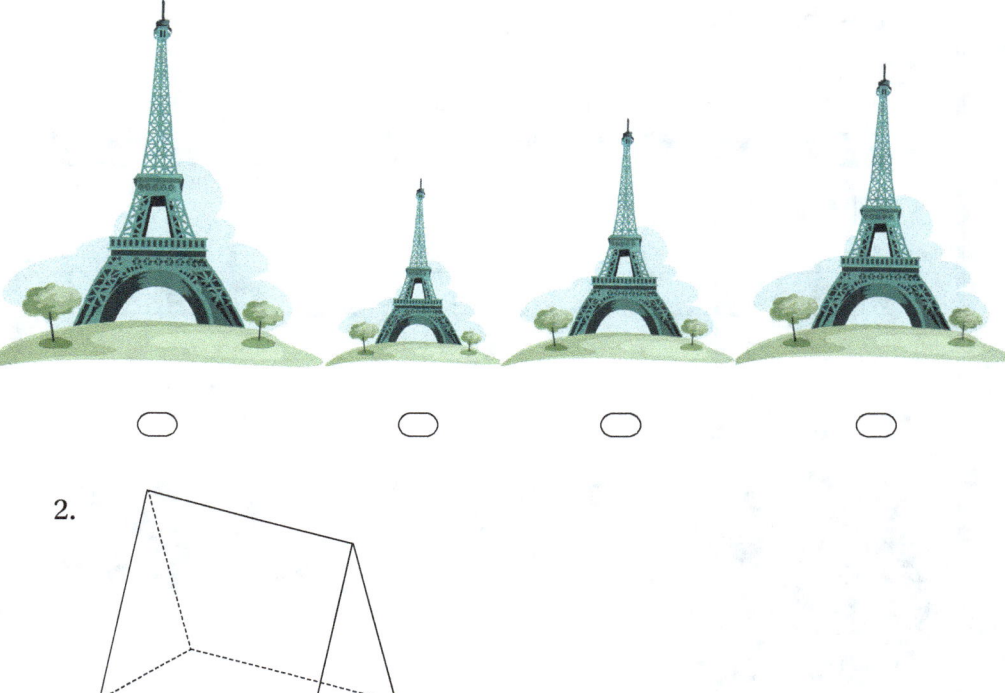

○   ○   ○   ○

2.

The name for the shape shown above is a

cube	triangle	triangular prism	triangular pyramid
○	○	○	○

3. This shows the number 10

   This shows the number 1

   Which number is shown by the following group of blocks?

   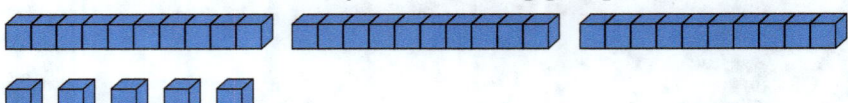

33	35	53	55
○	○	○	○

4. I have these coins to use.

   How much change would I get if I spent 35 cents?

5 cents	10 cents	15 cents	20 cents
○	○	○	○

5. Here is part of the calendar for April.

April						
Sunday						
		1	2	3	4	5
6	7	8	9	10	11	12

What day of the week is the 16th of April?

Sunday	Monday	Wednesday	Friday
○	○	○	○

6.

I have 24 flowers and I want to put 4 flowers in each vase. How many vases will I need?

3	5	6	8
○	○	○	○

7.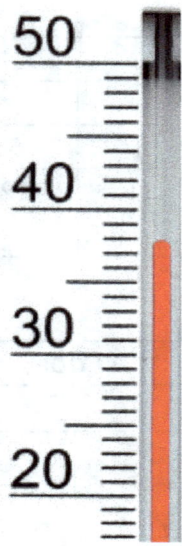

The reading on this thermometer is

17	30	38	40
○	○	○	○

8.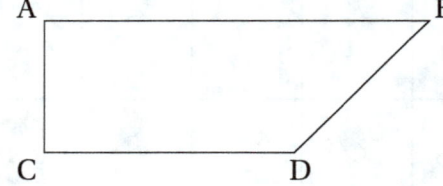

The biggest angle in the above shape is

A	B	C	D
○	○	○	○

9. 5 bunches of 4 bananas equals how many bananas?

10	16	20	24
○	○	○	○

10. Jane folds a piece of paper in half to get a shape like the one below.

She now cuts along the dotted line and then unfolds the paper.

Which one of the following is the shape formed?

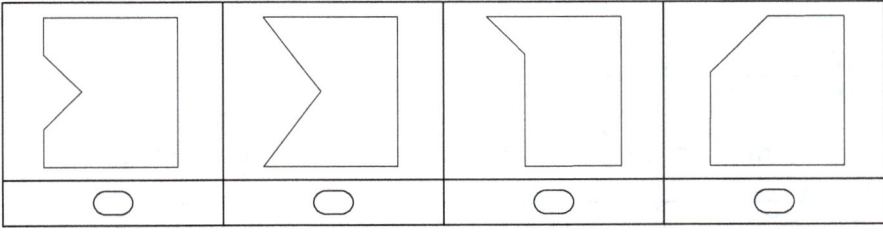

○	○	○	○

11.

	A	B	C	D	E
4					
3					
2					
1					

The square two squares to the right and one down from C3 is

E2	D2	D1	A2
○	○	○	○

12. Max can carry boxes weighing up to 32 kg. Which one of the following masses would be too heavy for him to carry?

53 kg	31 kg	12 kg	23 kg
○	○	○	○

13. Which letter would look the same after half a rotation (turn)?

D	H	L	E
○	○	○	○

14. The graph below shows the way children travel to school.

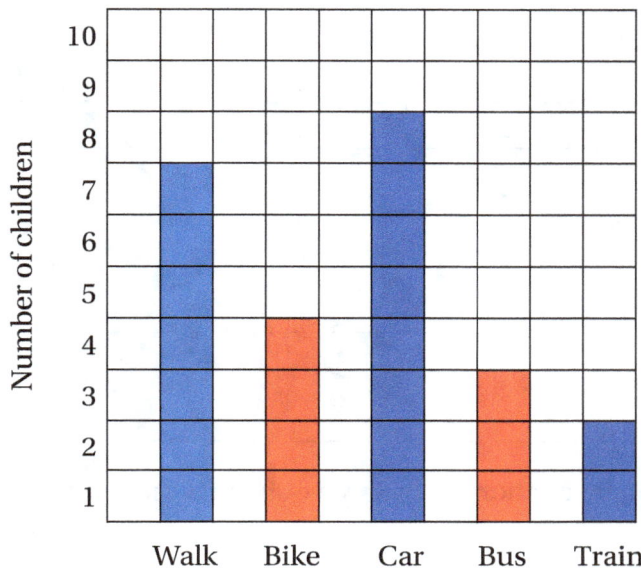

The total number of children who travel to school by bus or train is

2	3	4	5
○	○	○	○

15. The table below shows the number of students at the Happy Primary School who bought a particular drink on a certain day.

Drink	Number of students
Milk	39
Orange juice	75
Mineral water	102
Lemonade	
Total	240

How many of the students bought lemonade on this day?

23	24	25	34
○	○	○	○

16. Mario had 37 marbles but he lost 14 of them. How many did he have left?

23	24	25	33
○	○	○	○

17.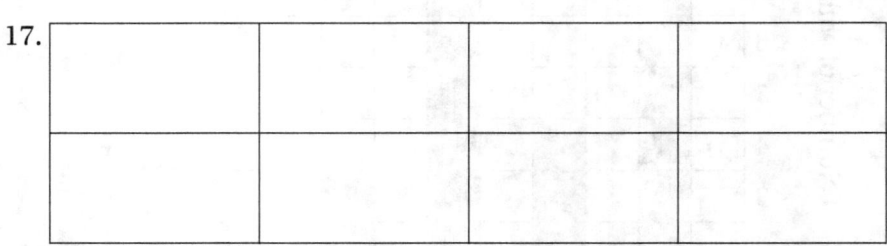

Which one of the fractions of the above shape is the greatest?

$\frac{1}{2}$	$\frac{1}{4}$	$\frac{1}{8}$	$\frac{3}{8}$
○	○	○	○

18.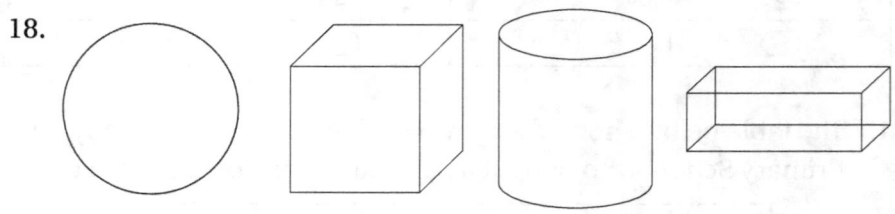

What is the name of the solid shape that is second from the right?

cube	rectangular prism	sphere	cylinder
○	○	○	○

19.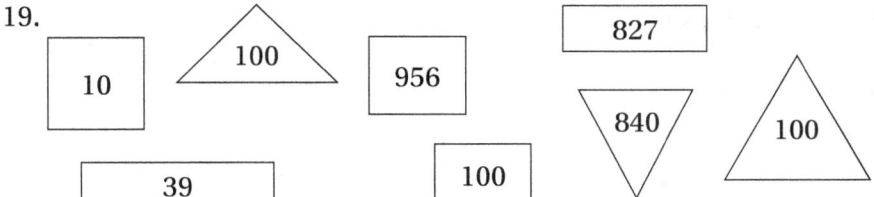

What is the answer when the numbers in the triangles are added together?

200	866	1,040	1,056
○	○	○	○

20.

What is the next symbol in the above pattern?

×	—	●	○
○	○	○	○

21. Which number is closest to 50?

45	49	55	59
○	○	○	○

22. Which clock shows the time 1:45 ?

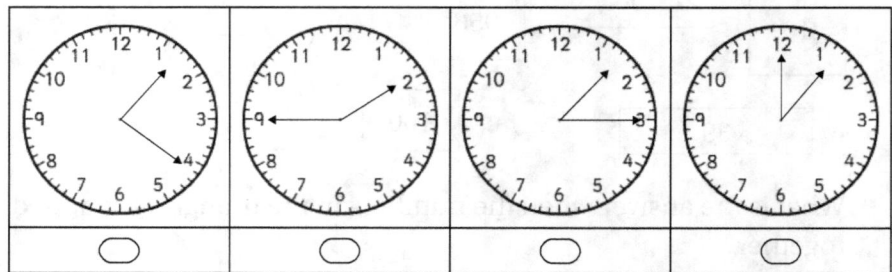

| ○ | ○ | ○ | ○ |

23. How many times will this shape

fit into this shape?

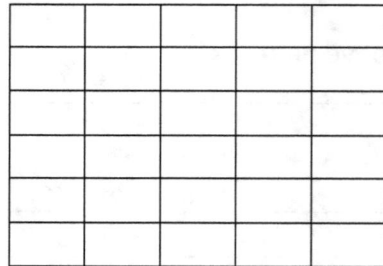

5	12	15	18
○	○	○	○

24. How many small cubes are needed to make this shape?

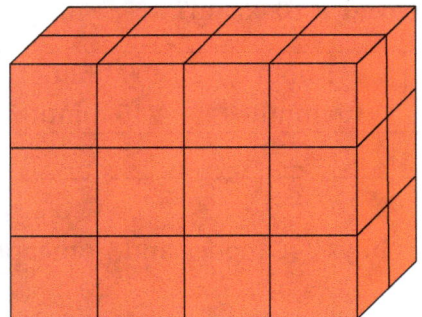

12	15	18	24
○	○	○	○

25. Sarah has 9 golf balls and she finds some more. She now has 22 golf balls.

How many did she find?

12	13	15	21
○	○	○	○

26.

•	• • •	• • • • • •	• • • • • • • • • •
1	3	6	10

1 , 3 , 6 , 10 are the first four triangular numbers. The next triangular number is

13	14	15	16
○	○	○	○

27. How long did Richard take to get to his grandmother's house if he left home at 9:30 am and arrived at 10:45 am?

45 minutes	1 hour	1 hour 15 minutes	1 hour 45 minutes
○	○	○	○

28. Mangoes cost $3.00 each. Maya buys 2 mangoes and 1 pineapple and pays $10.00.

    What is the cost of the pineapple?

$3.00	$4.00	$5.00	$6.00
○	○	○	○

29.
Z	Y	X

     | W | V | U |

When this net is made into a cube, which face will be opposite the face marked **Y**?

V	W	X	U
○	○	○	○

30. 35, 48, 61, 74, . . .

    What is the next number in this pattern?

31. How much change will Molly get from $10.00 if she buys a loaf of bread for $3.25 and a drink for $2.30?

$ ⬚

32. 135 can be written as

13 ones and 5 tens	1 ten and 35 ones	1 hundred and 35 tens	13 tens and 5 ones
○	○	○	○

33. Abby, Ben and Cate have 26 lollies altogether. They want to have 8 lollies each, and then give any that are left over to Cate's little sister, Jess.

How many lollies will they give to Jess?

34.

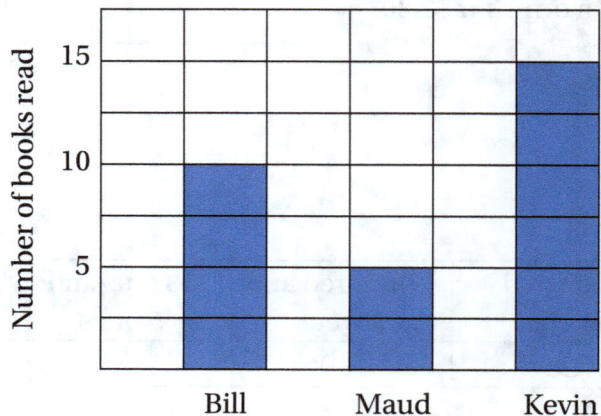

The above graph shows the number of books read by Bill, Maud and Kevin. Which statement is true?

◯ Kevin read twice the number of books that Maud read.

◯ Bill and Maud together read twice the number of books that Kevin read.

◯ Maud and Kevin together read twice the number of books that Bill read.

◯ Bill and Maud together read more books than Kevin.

35. Gary has 13 more Smarties than Meg. Finn has 25 more Smarties than Meg. Gary has 56 Smarties.

How many Smarties does Finn have?

Answers

Writing

Here is a sample writing response for the **narrative** prompt.

The Note

The wizard asked me if I wanted seeds for a giant beanstalk.

I said no. He told me he also had seeds for ice cream trees or money plants.

"I'll have the money plant seeds, please," I said.

He said, "Plant the seeds in the sun and water them every day."

I asked Dad, "Where can I plant my seeds?"

Dad said, "Over near the fence. What are they?"

He laughed when I told him they were money plant seeds.

"Give me the first flower," he said.

Every day I put water on the seeds.

After six weeks I saw bits of green. In August, I got my ruler and saw that the plants were ten centimetres high.

In September, they were fourteen centimeters high.

Then, in October, there was some purple among the green.

It was the first flower!

When it was a proper rectangle I picked it.

I wrote on a yellow sticky note to Dad and put it on the money with a paper clip.

When Dad came home from work I gave him the $5.

He read the note.

> To Dad. Here is the first flower from my money plants.
> Love from Tom

Dad fainted.

Here is a sample writing response for the **persuasive** prompt.

A cat makes a better pet than a dog

Burglars, walks and fun mean that a cat is not a better pet than a dog.

If a burglar comes to your house and there is no one at home, your dog will stop the burglar getting in. Most dogs bark and sound bigger than they are. Even though you know your pet will not bite, the burglar doesn't. It will scare the burglar away. Cats don't bark.

After school and on weekends, we have to take our dog for a walk. It is good exercise for us and the dog. We can practise our throwing for cricket and baseball as our dog loves to follow the ball and bring it back. I have not seen cats walking or running after balls on our beach.

At home, we have fun trying to teach our dog tricks. Sometimes it will roll over or sit up and beg. It looks so funny that we laugh and laugh. It is much more fun than a cat.

For our family, our dog gives us exercise, fun and keeps us safe.

For us, a dog is a better pet than a cat.

Reading

What we did during the holidays...

1. **During the holidays, which children went to the beach?**
    - ○ Susie and Jane
    - ○ Jack and Mitchell
    - ○ Mitchell and Susie
    - ● Susie and Jack

    Susie and Jack *is the correct answer. We can read this in the text when Susie says that she went to her grandma's beach house. Jack replies by saying that he also went to the beach.*

2. **Why did Jack get sore feet?**
    - ○ from playing games at Kids' Club
    - ○ because he tripped over
    - ○ from swimming
    - ● from walking on broken shells

    From walking on broken shells *is the correct answer. Jack tells us this when he says: 'There were broken shells all over the sand, which made our feet sore...'*

3. **From reading the text, which child do we know saw a movie during the holidays?**
   - ● Jane
   - ○ Jack
   - ○ Susie
   - ○ Mitchell

   Jane is the correct answer. She is the only child in the text to say that she went to the movies.

4. **Where is the zoo?**
   - ○ at the beach
   - ● in the Botanical Gardens
   - ○ in the city
   - ○ far away

   ***In the Botanical Gardens** is the correct answer. In the text, Mitchell says that he went to the Botanical Gardens Zoo.*

5. **From reading the text, which of the children does not seem to have a brother or sister?**
   - ○ Susie
   - ● Jane
   - ○ Mitchell
   - ○ Jack

   Jane is the correct answer. In their stories, Susie, Jack and Mitchell all mention a brother or sister. Jane is the only child in the text that does not talk about a brother or sister.

6. **How do we know that Jack and Susie did not go to the same beach?**

    ○ Susie did not go to a beach

    ● the beach that Susie went to was far away

    ○ Jack did not go to a beach

    ○ because of the seaweed

The beach that Susie went to was far away is the correct answer. In the text, Susie explains that her grandma's beach house was a long drive away. Jack explains that the beach he went to was not far away. This means that they could not have gone to the same beach.

Turtles

7. **Turtles have lived on Earth for how many million years?**

    ○ 250

    ○ 225

    ○ 300

    ● 220

220 is the correct answer. The first paragraph tells us this information.

8. **Turtles are**

    ○ fish

    ● reptiles

    ○ plants

    ○ insects

Reptiles is the correct answer. The first sentence states that turtles are reptiles.

9. **Where might you *not* find a turtle?**
    - ○ in a swamp
    - ○ in saltwater
    - ● in a desert
    - ○ in a fishpond

    In a desert *is the correct answer. The text tells us that turtles live in all kinds of water. Deserts do not have water.*

10. **The text does not tell us that turtles like to eat**
    - ○ bugs
    - ○ leaves
    - ○ small fish
    - ● birds

    Birds *is the correct answer. The text states in the final sentence that turtles like to eat fish, plants and insects (bugs). It does not state that turtles like to eat birds.*

11. **How are turtles different from tortoises?**
    - ○ tortoises can be pets
    - ○ tortoises like the water
    - ○ tortoises generally live in the sea
    - ● tortoises don't live in the water

    Tortoises don't live in the water *is the correct answer. In the second paragraph, the text tells us that turtles are different from tortoises in that tortoises generally live on land.*

12. **A turtle would make a good pet because**
    - ○ they need lots of space
    - ● they live in water
    - ○ they are expensive
    - ○ they are difficult to feed

    They live in water *is the best answer because the text mentions that 'some people keep turtles as pets' and earlier establishes that turtles live in water environments.*

The ant and the dove

13. **What word could be used to describe the bank of the river instead of *slick*?**
    - ○ dry
    - ● slippery
    - ○ sticky
    - ○ grassy

    Slippery *is the correct answer. We can tell the bank was 'slippery' because the ant slipped into the river.*

14. **What word best describes the dove in this story?**
    - ○ coward
    - ● hero
    - ○ bully
    - ○ tease

    Hero *is the best answer because the dove saved the ant from drowning. Coward, bully and tease do not fit well as answers.*

15. **Why did the ant bite the man on the toe?**

    ○ the man made the ant fall in the river

    ○ the ant was afraid

    ○ the ant did not like people

    ● the ant wanted to save the dove

    The ant wanted to save the dove *is the best answer. The story tells us that the ant bit the man on the toe when the ant saw that the man was trying to hurt the dove.*

16. **In the beginning of the story, what word could best be used in place of *parched*?**

    ○ angry

    ○ refreshed

    ● thirsty

    ○ cool

    Thirsty *is the correct answer. From the story, we can tell that parched can mean thirsty. The first sentence tells us that the ant was parched and the next sentence in the story tells us that the ant bent down to get a drink.*

17. **In the story, the ant is '*floundering for his life*'. This means the ant is**

    ○ running for his life

    ○ fighting with the dove

    ○ fighting with the man

    ● trying not to drown

    Trying not to drown *is the correct answer. The ant cannot be running, or fighting with the dove or the man, because the ant is in the water.*

18. **What do you think is the message to be taken from this story?**
    - kind acts are repaid
    ○ ants can drown
    ○ men do not like doves
    ○ rivers are dangerous

Kind acts are repaid is the best answer because the most important part of the story is that the dove saves the ant, which is a kind act, and the ant then saves the dove in return.

Onion tears

19. **The children did not use**
    ○ red paint
    - blue paint
    ○ green paint
    ○ orange paint

Blue paint is the correct answer. The story tells us that the children used red, green and orange paint.

20. **From reading the story, who can we guess is the best at painting?**
    ○ Mary
    ○ Danny
    - the storyteller
    ○ Tessa

The storyteller is likely to be the best painter because the storyteller paints the difficult pictures like the butterflies and the dragon. Tessa and Mary just paint colours on their bikes and Danny does not paint at all.

21. **Where on the bikes did the storyteller paint butterflies?**
    - ● the mudguards
    - ○ the handlebars
    - ○ the wheels
    - ○ the spokes

    The mudguards *is the answer. The storyteller tells us in the second paragraph that she paints butterflies on the mudguards.*

22. **The storyteller tells us that Danny '*stuck hundreds of stickers everywhere*'. This means that Danny put stickers**
    - ○ all over Mary's house
    - ○ all over the ground
    - ● all over his bike
    - ○ all over the storyteller

    All over his bike *is the best answer. The story is about the children decorating their bikes.*

23. **Which kind of stickers did Danny *not* put on his bike?**
    - ○ pop star stickers
    - ○ football stickers
    - ● dragon stickers
    - ○ funny face stickers

    Dragon stickers *is the correct answer. The text tells us that the storyteller* painted *a dragon on Danny's bike and that Danny put pop star, football and funny face stickers on his bike.*

24. **At the end of the text, the storyteller whispers the meaning of her name to Mary only. Which of the following *best* explains why?**

   ○ Tessa and Danny don't ride bikes

   ○ she does not like Tessa and Danny

   ● she only wants Mary to know

   ○ Danny and Tessa do not like the storyteller

*When the storyteller whispers only to Mary, this suggests that **she only wants Mary to know**. The story tells us that Danny and Tessa have bikes, which suggests that they do ride bikes and the story does not at all suggest that some of the children do not like one another.*

Shane Gould, golden girl

25. **How old was Shane when she won her first silver medal?**

   ○ ten

   ● nine

   ○ fifteen

   ○ fourteen

***Nine** is the correct answer. The text tells us that Shane won her first silver medal when she was nine years old.*

26. **Shane's '*arm strokes were exact and powerful*'. What word could be used instead of *powerful*?**

    ○ weak

    ○ deep

    ● strong

    ○ light

    Strong *is the correct answer. Strong is the only word in this group that has a similar meaning to the word powerful. None of the other answers fit well in place of the word powerful.*

27. **The text tells us that '*swimming was Shane's life*'. This tells us that Shane**

    ○ didn't like swimming

    ○ swam in her sleep

    ● loved swimming

    ○ sort of liked swimming

    Loved swimming *is the correct answer. 'Swam in her sleep,' 'didn't like swimming' and 'sort of liked swimming' are all incorrect answers.*

28. **Shane was the youngest Australian Olympic medallist in history. This means that**

    ○ no one this young was allowed to win before

    ● Shane was the first Australian this young to win

    ○ Shane won many medals

    ○ Shane was the first person in the world to ever win

    Shane was the first Australian this young to win *is the correct answer. The first and the last answers are completely incorrect and 'Shane won many medals,' though true, does not correctly complete the sentence.*

29. **When the starting gun went off, Shane *'cut the water like a knife'*. This means that Shane**
    - ○ used a knife to cut the water
    - ○ dove into the water roughly
    - ● went through the water sharply
    - ○ swam really slowly

    Went through the water sharply *is the correct answer. From reading the text we can tell that Shane did not use an actual knife to cut the water, nor did she dive roughly or swim slowly.*

30. **'*Shane took the lead and held it.*' What does this mean?**
    - ○ Shane grabbed a hold of the ropes
    - ● Shane was winning all along
    - ○ the other swimmers caught up to Shane
    - ○ the other swimmers let her win

    Shane was winning all along *is the correct answer. The text does not indicate that Shane grabbed hold of the rope; that the other swimmers caught up to Shane; or that the other swimmers let Shane win the race.*

Orangutan

31. **The text describes Orangutans as *arboreal*. This means that orangutans**
    - ○ live in caves
    - ○ live in captivity
    - ● live in trees
    - ○ are not real

    Live in trees *is the correct answer. The text states that 'Orangutans are arboreal, which means that they live in trees...'*

32. **Male orangutans**
    - ○ live in groups
    - ○ stay in the trees
    - ● are solitary
    - ○ weigh about 100 kilograms

    Are solitary *is the correct answer. The text states that 'males are largely solitary creatures.'*

33. **Orangutans are an *endangered* species. This means that orangutans**
    - ○ are dangerous
    - ○ are kept in captivity
    - ● are in danger
    - ○ are lonely

    Are in danger *is the correct answer. The text tells us that orangutans are 'endangered because their habitats are being destroyed and because they have been hunted and sold as pets.' Also, the other answers are not appropriate.*

34. **In Sumatra and Kalimantan some orangutans are kept in rehabilitation centres. They are kept in these centres**
    - ○ to be sold later as pets
    - ○ to learn to be nomadic
    - ● to learn survival skills
    - ○ to protect humans

    To learn survival skills *is the correct answer. The text tells us that orangutans kept in rehabilitation centres 'are taught the skills they need to survive in the wild.'*

35. **Orangutans do *not* eat**
    - ○ leaves
    - ○ birds' eggs
    - ○ insects
    - ● birds

    Birds *is the correct answer. The text tells us that orangutans like to eat leaves, birds' eggs and insects. 'Birds' eggs' means the eggs of birds and not the birds themselves.*

36. **Which of the following statements about orangutans is *incorrect***
    - ○ males usually weigh more
    - ○ females usually stay up in the trees
    - ○ orangutans only have one enemy
    - ● females usually give birth to lots of young

    Females usually give birth to lots of young *is the incorrect statement. The text tells us that they usually give birth to only 'one, but sometimes two, young.'*

Language conventions

Spelling

The spelling mistakes in these sentences have been circled. Write the correct spelling for each circled word in the box.

1. His shirt is made of (coton.) | 1. cotton

2. Please (cloze) the door. | 2. close

3. Jenna went (shoping) today. | 3. shopping

4. We waited (abowt) an hour for the bus. | 4. about

5. Mum (parkt) the car. | 5. parked

6. Suki doesn't like (lizerds.) | 6. lizards

7. Possums like eating (appels.) | 7. apples

8. Everyone thinks Anna is (pritty)   8. pretty

9. Brendon (kiked) the ball.   9. kicked

10. Peter is (cuming) to my party.   10. coming

The spelling mistakes on these labels have been circled. Write the correct spelling for each circled word in the box.

13. long (wiskers)

whiskers

14. padded (pors)

paws

11. big (tale)

tail

12. black (strips) of fur

stripes

Anna

Each line has one word that is incorrect.
Write the correct spelling of the word in the box.

15. Anna coud not wait until her next

could

16. birthday becorse her mum had

because

17. promist to get her some new

promised

18. cloths. She was very excited.

clothes

Cows

Each line has one word that is incorrect.
Write the correct spelling of the word in the box.

19. By makeing milk to have for

making

20. our brekfast, cows are very

breakfast

21. useful animels on cattle farms. | animals |

The Visit

**Each line has one word that is incorrect.
Write the correct spelling of the word in the box.**

22. My parrents have been waiting | parents |

23. a very long time for my unkle to | uncle |

24. visit us. They allways talk about him | always |

25. and are exited to see him again. | excited |

Grammar and punctuation

26. Which of the following correctly completes the sentence?

   Penny is _____ by the window.

sit	sitting	sat	sitted
○	●	○	○

27. Which of the following correctly completes the sentence?

   Dad threw the ball at _____ .

she	hers	herself	her
○	○	○	●

28. Which of the following correctly completes the sentence?

   I am going to Devon's house _____ .

yesterday	tomorrow	last Saturday	before today
○	●	○	○

29. Shade one bubble to show where the missing comma (,) should go.

   Jo likes steak chips and salad for dinner.
   ○ ● ○ ○

30. Which of the following correctly completes the sentence?

   The dinner will be cooked _____ an hour.

on	with	at	in
○	○	○	●

31. Shade one bubble to show where the missing full stop (.) should go.

Jess had a blue and yellow bike Jenny thought it looked very nice.
    ○   ●   ○   ○

32. Which of the following correctly completes the sentence?

He leaned his bike _____ the wall.

against	on	into	over
●	○	○	○

33. Which of the following correctly completes the sentence?

The book, _____ was green, belonged to the library.

who	what	which	why
○	○	●	○

34. Which of the following has the correct punctuation?

● John is ten years old. He reads magazines about cars.

○ John is ten years old he reads magazines about cars.

○ John is ten years old. He reads magazines. About cars.

○ John is ten years old. he reads magazines about cars.

The writing below has some gaps.
Choose the best option to fill in each of the gaps.
Shade the bubble to show your answer.

35. Everything is beautiful in the summer ○ . ● , ○ ? ○ !

36. except ___ the flies. No matter how ○ with ● for ○ in ○ to

37. hard I try to keep ___ out of the house ● them ○ it ○ they ○ those

38. they manage to sneak ___ . I only have to ○ out ○ up ● in ○ about

39. open the door ___ a minute and an army ○ with ○ in ○ at ● for

40. of flies ___ buzzing in my kitchen. ● is ○ be ○ am ○ are

41. Which of the following correctly completes the sentence?

I have borrowed _____ pencil.

Jennys	Jenny's	Jennys'	Jenny's'
○	●	○	○

42. Which sentence has the correct punctuation?

● Do you like chocolate flavour?
○ Do you, like chocolate flavour?
○ Do you like chocolate flavour.
○ Do you like, chocolate flavour?

43. Which of the following correctly completes the sentence?

I have _____ to him before.

speak	spoke	spoken	speaked
○	○	●	○

44. Which of the following correctly completes the sentence?

I _____ living in my house for three years.

am	been	have been	were
○	○	●	○

45. Which sentence has the correct punctuation?

● Jane, who is a tennis player, is very athletic.
○ Jane who, is a tennis player, is very athletic.
○ Jane who is a tennis player is very, athletic.
○ Jane who is a tennis player, is very athletic.

46. Which of the following correctly completes the sentence?

The movie _____ already.

has begun	began	was began	have begun
●	○	○	○

47. Which of the following correctly completes the sentence?

This cake tastes _____ better than that one.

more	most	many	much
○	○	○	●

48. Which of the following correctly completes the sentence?

He had an _____ for lunch.

banana	sandwich	noodle	apple
○	○	○	●

49. Which sentence is correct?

○ She and its brother went to the cinema.

● She and her brother went to the cinema.

○ Her and his brother went to the cinema.

○ She and him went to the cinema.

50. Shade one bubble to show where the missing speech mark (") should go.

○   ○   ●   ○
↓   ↓   ↓   ↓

"Wait a minute, it's my turn first, interrupted Jade.

Language conventions answers in detail

Questions 1–25 are spelling mistakes.

Question 26: The gerund *sitting* has to be used with the present tense auxiliary *to be* to form the present progressive tense.

Question 27: The sentence requires a direct object for the verb, and the third person object pronoun is *her*. (*She* is a subject pronoun, *hers* is possessive pronoun, and *herself* is a reflexive pronoun.)

Question 28: The only adverbial suitable for a present progressive tense is *tomorrow* – the others are all past tense markers.

Question 29: The comma comes after *steak* because it is a list. It is not appropriate anywhere else because as a simple sentence it contains a single clause.

Question 30: The only appropriate preposition in Standard English is *in*.

Question 31: The full stop is used to separate the two sentences, each containing a single clause.

Question 32: The only appropriate preposition in Standard English is *against*.

Question 33: A relative pronoun is required here, so *what* and *why* (interrogative pronouns) cannot be used, and *who* is used to refer to people, so *which* is the only correct answer.

Question 34: The full stop is used to separate the two sentences, each containing a single clause, beginning with a capital letter.

Question 35: A comma is appropriate here because the sentence is not complete, and the following word does not begin with a capital letter (which would be the case with the other punctuation options). The comma emphasizes the contrast provided by the preposition.

Question 36: *For* is the only appropriate preposition in Standard English.

Question 37: The pronoun is replacing *flies*, so it has to be a third person plural form, which discounts *it*. The pronoun here functions as the object of the sentence, so it had to be the object pronoun *them*. *Those* is discounted because it is a demonstrative pronoun.

Question 38: *In* is the only appropriate preposition to complete the verb phrase in this context in Standard English.

Question 39: *For* is the only appropriate preposition in Standard English.

Question 40: The third person singular form of the verb *to be* is the right answer because *army* is a collective noun and takes a singular verb.

Question 41: The *pencil* belongs grammatically to *Jenny*, and so this word needs the addition of the singular possessive inflection: *'s* (*Jenny's*).

Question 42: The sentence is interrogative (question) so requires a question mark, and the sentence must begin with a capital letter.

Question 43: The past participle of *speak* is *spoken*, which is required in forming the perfect tense.

Question 44: The past participle of *be* is *been*, but this requires an auxiliary to make the past perfect tense, which this sentence requires. The other two options are inappropriate because *am* is present tense, and *were* is the simple past tense in its plural form.

Question 45: *Who is a tennis player* is the relative clause that has been embedded in the main clause *Jane is very athletic*, and so therefore needs surrounding by the commas.

Question 46: The sentence requires the perfect tense, requiring the appropriate form of the auxiliary *to have* and the past participle of *begin*, which is *begun*. *Began* is the simple past tense, and *was begun* is the past progressive, so these answers are inappropriate. *Movie* is singular so requires *has* as the auxiliary, thus: *the movie has begun already* is the correct answer.

Question 47: *Much* is the only appropriate adverbial intensifier because better is a comparative adjective so cannot be modified by the comparative *more* or the superlative *most*. *More* is an adjective and cannot be used as an adverb.

Question 48: The noun that follows the indefinite article *an* has to begin with a vowel.

Question 49: The sentence requires the subject pronoun *she* as *she* is the subject of the sentence. *Her* is the possessive pronoun that suggests the brother belongs to *she*. (Technically this is not strictly speaking a possessive pronoun, but rather functions as a possessive adjective to modify the word *brother*).

Question 50: The closing speech mark goes at the end of the utterance.

Numeracy

1. Smallest means shortest. **The second from the left.**
2. This shape is a prism because you can cut slices parallel to the triangular base that would all be the same. It is a **triangular prism** because the base is a triangle.
3. We have 10 + 10 + 10 + 1 + 1 + 1 + 1 + 1 = 35 or 3 tens and 5 ones = **35**
4. I have 45 cents. If I spend 35 cents I have 45 − 35 = **10 cents change**.
5. Put the days of the week in order in the top row and put the numbers in order up to 16. The 16th will occur under **Wednesday**.
6. Group the flowers in fours. The number of groups is **6**.
7. Each horizontal line represents 1. The top of the thermometer reading is 8 marks above 30 which is **38**.
8. A and C are each 90°. B is acute, D is obtuse. Hence, **D** is the largest angle.
9. 5 lots of 4 = 5 × 4 = **20**
10. When you open the paper you will get an indented triangular shape which will not start at the bottom of the rectangle. Hence, **the shape on the left of the answers**.
11. Two squares to the right → is E3 and then one down ↓ is **E2**.
12. 53 is bigger than 32, so **53 kg** would be too heavy for Max.
13. With half a turn, **H would look the same.** D, L and E would look back to front, as if they had been flipped over a vertical line.
14. 3 travel by bus and 2 travel by train, so the total who travel by bus or train = 2 + 3 = **5**.
15. 39 + 75 + 102 = 216 bought drinks other than lemonade.

    Number who bought lemonade = 240 − 216 = **24**.

16. 37 − 14 = **23**
17. $\frac{1}{2}$ **is the greatest.**

    $\frac{1}{2}$ is 4 rectangles. $\frac{1}{4}$ is 2 rectangles. $\frac{1}{8}$ is 1 rectangle. $\frac{3}{8}$ is 3 rectangles.
18. The sphere is on the left and the rectangular prism is on the right. **Second from the right is the cylinder.**
19. △ is a triangle.

    Numbers in the triangles added = 100 + 840 + 100 = 1,040.
20. Every third shape is the symbol inside the previous shape, so ──
21. When we count **49 is next to 50**. 49 is one less than 50, 45 is 5 less than 50, 55 is 5 more than 50, 59 is 9 more than 50.
22. 1:45 is a quarter to 2. The little hand has almost reached 2 and the big hand is on the 9. **The second clock from the left in the answers.**
23. 3 of the small shape can fit in one column of the big shape. There are 5 columns so 3 lots of 5 = 3 × 5 = **15**.
24. Need 12 for the front layer and 12 for the back layer = **24**.
25. 22 − 9 = **13**.
26. The next triangular number has 5 dots in the bottom line as well as the 10 dots from the previous number = 10 + 5 = **15**.
27. At 10:30 it would be 1 hour. Another 15 minutes to reach 10:45, so **1 hour 15 minutes**.
28. Maya's mangoes cost $6.00. Pineapple costs $10.00 − $6.00 = **$4.00**.
29. W will be the base, X will come up the side and Y and Z will wrap around to make sides so that Z is opposite X, and **V is opposite Y**. U will be the top opposite W.

30. Each number is 13 more than the previous number. 74 + 13 = **87**

31. Bread and drink cost $3.25 + $2.30 = $5.55.
    Change = $10.00 − $5.55 = **$4.45**.

32. 135 is 1 hundred, 3 tens and 5 ones. 1 hundred is 10 tens.
    So 135 = **13 tens and 5 ones**.

33. Abby gets 8, Ben gets 8 and Cate gets 8. This is 24 lollies altogether which leaves 26 − 24 = **2 lollies for Jess**.

34. Bill read 10 books, Maud read 5 books and Kevin read 15 books. Maud and Kevin together read 20 books. **Maud and Kevin together read twice the number of books that Bill read.**

35. Meg has 56 − 13 = 43 Smarties. Finn has 43 + 25 = 68 Smarties.

www.ingramcontent.com/pod-product-compliance
Lightning Source LLC
Chambersburg PA
CBHW050306120526
44590CB00016B/2508